ns
The Pe...

How to Experience an... ...e Peace of God Through Fear, Chaos, Troubles, and Anxiety.

Leon O. Newman © Text 2021

All rights Reserved.

No part of this publication may be reproduced, distributed, or transmitted in any form or by any means, including photocopying, recording, or other electronic or mechanical methods, without the prior written permission of the publisher

Except in the case of brief quotations embodied in critical reviews and certain other noncommercial uses permitted by copyright law.

Scriptural Quotations

The information offered here is for the purposes of spiritual upliftment and growth only. The author is aware that the application of this book many differ from one person to another as such things as faith, persistency, trust, and love for God can determine the outcomes that you receive from the application of the principles in this book.

Unless otherwise indicated, all scriptural quotations are taken from the New King James Version © 1988-2007 Bible Soft Inc.

Scriptural quotation indicated RSV is taken from the Revised Standard Version of the Bible, Copyright © 1946, 1952, and 1971 used with Permission.

TABLE OF CONTENT

FREE GIFT 4

Introduction: Enjoying the peace of God 5

Chapter One: Acknowledge God in your life 14

Chapter Two: Ask God for His peace 22

Chapter Three: Stand on God's promises 30

Chapter Four: Submit to God's Will 38

Chapter Five: Trust in God always 46

Chapter Six: Flee from Sin 54

Chapter Seven: Seek the Favor of God 62

Chapter Eight: Pursue Peace 70

Chapter Nine: Act peacefully 80

Chapter Ten: Believe in God 84

ABOUT THE AUTHOR 93

ONE LAST THING 94

FREE BOOK

HOW IS YOUR **THINKING?**

Remaining resilient in the face of negative and challenging circumstances requires an intentional mindset shift. This book acts as a guidance and reminder to you, that you are a magnificent, extraordinary expression of awesomeness. You are worth it. You are important. You are strong. You are handsome. You are beautiful. You are smart. You are successful. You are loved. You are more than you could ever imagine.

Download this powerful book today for free

VISIT

www.iampurposeful.org/free

TO DOWNLOAD

Introduction

Enjoying the peace of God

The world is filled with chaos, turmoil, and confusion, most times leaving us with a myriad of psychosocial, emotional, and physical problems. The kind of peace like the world will gift you is fleeting. It comes and goes in a breeze.

John 14: 27:

"Peace I leave with you, my peace I give unto you: not as the world giveth, give I unto you. Let not your heart be troubled, neither let it be afraid."

Have you just been free from financial burden yesterday

and heave a sigh of relief that you have your peace, but unfortunately, the next day, you encounter the next financial burden that is giving you sleepless nights? The peace that God promised you isn't of the world.

Then you may ask what is God kind of peace is? In the scriptures, the God kind of peace he wants for you is the peace that transcends all understanding. It is simply about the calm and harmony of the body, spirit, and mind that surpass earthly understanding and circumstances (Philippians 4:7).

John 16:33:

"These things I have spoken unto you, that in me ye might have peace. In the world ye shall have tribulation: but be of good cheer; I have overcome the world."

The truth is that a peace-loving God can only give peace to his loving children, which you are one of them. If you believe that everything about God is peaceful, then acknowledging this alone should steer you in the path of peace only. This is where you should get it right; as long as you are in the world, you will be confronted with tribulations (debt, losses, failures, sorrows, etc.) that will take away your peace, but you can have the peace that comes with blessings from only God.

You can describe God kind of peace as a tranquil state of faith and appreciation, and it can be gotten when you submit totally to God's commandments and trust. Experiencing God's peace will need you to be humble and courageous, which will enable you to look beyond the mere abilities of your understanding — to trust that God is leading you in the path that you should go. The less you try to grasp it with your understanding, the better it is to allow your heart to align with what God has prepared for you (Proverbs 3: 5).

One person that enjoyed the peace of God as promised was King David.

2 Samuel 7:1-3:

"And it came to pass, when the king sat in his house, and the Lord had given him rest roundabout from all his enemies;

2 That the king said unto Nathan the prophet, see now, I dwell in a house of cedar, but the ark of God dwelleth within curtains.

3 And Nathan said to the king, Go, do all that is in thine heart; for the Lord is with thee."

You can deduce from this scripture that David was enjoying an unusual season of peace from God. He was given rest, which is a peace of mind from his enemies.

You might think that there cannot be the peace you desired where there is turbulence but always remember with God, you can experience it and more in abundance. You love a time of peace in your life, or don't you? Then you don't need to be dismayed when you are confronted by pains, grief, pressure, stress, heartache, and all kinds of aches. God's words are yea and Amen.

John 16:33:

"These things I have spoken unto you, that in me ye might have peace. In the world ye shall have tribulation: but be of good cheer; I have overcome the world."

This scripture simply means that God has promised you His kind of peace and rest, and you shouldn't be troubled at all despite your present situations. If you are in God, you will surely enter his place of rest.

I remember years back when the facilitator in my local assembly gave us a little insight into his own life as a person. He said he grew up in a polygamous home full of fights, unhealthy competition, jealousy, and lack of love. It was really an unpleasant and unstable atmosphere that peace wasn't given a chance at all.

Members of the family took to wayward lifestyles, anger, and all kind of abuses. But what helped was that he took responsibility for all his actions and sought God wholeheartedly. He said he realized that getting aggravated, angry, worried, or frustrated will do no good; instead, it will bring more sleepless time and total lack of peace. He invited God into his life and asked for his peace like a river. He began to experience the peace that dwells from his inside. The peace God gives to you will touch every fiber of your being, and that's the truth.

Isaiah 66:12:

"For thus saith the Lord, Behold, I will extend peace to her like a river, and the glory of the Gentiles like a flowing stream: then shall ye suck, ye shall be borne upon her sides, and be dandled upon her knees."

This scripture tells us that God will direct peace to you, just like a river, and it will never run dry. The Word of God is interesting; it uses the environment to give you insights. Have you ever been to a river? It is always peaceful. Experiencing God's peace is forever, and you don't need to go looking for it because it will come or locate you without much stress.

Experiencing God's peace is important in a chaotic world like ours. You should know that experiencing God's peace comes with its gift like harmony, fulfillment, contentment, order, etc. The reasons you should seek to experience God's peace will be of immense essence to you. God knows the benefits you will derive from wrapping yourself in His peace. What are the things that take away the peace of God in your heart? Let them go. Seek what brings peace to your life (Psalm 34; 14). You are not only to seek it but to diligently go after it, so that you wouldn't be prevented from enjoying the fruits of living permanently in God's peace. You will enjoy the following when you are enjoying God's peace.

FAVOR WITH GOD AND WITH MEN

You will find favor before God and man because nobody will want to favor a troublesome person. If you are enjoying the peace that is in Christ Jesus, then nothing will trouble you or having the negative spirit of troubling others. Look around you and realize that most peaceful people are being blessed daily by people in their workplace, on the road, in their business, etc.

When you are experiencing the peace of God, you will be highly favored.

YOU DISPLAY YOUR SONSHIP

As a son of God, whenever you display peace amidst chaotic circumstances, you act like your Father in Heaven.

Mathew 5:9:

"Blessed are the peacemakers: for they shall be called the children of God."

When you are experiencing God's peace automatically, you will only exude peace because you can only give what you have. Being a peacemaker comes with the blessing of being called a child of God.

When you become a child of God, you should only expect the best of gifts from God. God has revealed in his words that the thoughts He has for you are thoughts to give you peace, not thoughts that will bring you distress or evil, but thoughts to give you an expected life bubbling end.

PEACE OF MIND

A lot of issues, challenges, and problems emanate from a lack of peace. Lack of good health, psychological, emotional, and mental health is among problems that one can encounter from lacking peace of mind. Have you ever had your mind in so many places? Tuition fees, rent payment, emotional distress, workplace pressure, etc. It can not only be drowning but also draining. You will enjoy peace of mind when you experience God's kind of peace.

Proverbs 16:7:

"When a man's ways please the Lord, he maketh even his enemies to be at peace with him."

See anything that will take away your peace of mind as an enemy.

God can only restore your peace of mind. God takes pleasure in you when you are in his peace and bring you nothing else than wholeness, which is your peace of mind. The enemies or problems that have stolen your peace; God is making them be at peace with you right now.

There is a lot you will benefit from experiencing total

peace, which can only come from God. Peace is your win as a child of God. Believe that you have God's peace. Taking this action will see you living the life of wholesomeness, and this is what you need to stay sane in a world as crazy as we have here. Life will be dotted with all manners of issues if you do not abide in the peace of God. The truth is that experiencing God's peace has been freely given to you by God. So, if you are ready to experience God's kind of peace, then you stick around as I take you through the little things you will do to get there. Keep enmeshing in God's only peace.

Chapter One

Acknowledge God in your life

The truth is that you can have all the luxuries life has got to offer, but without having peace, you can't truly enjoy your life, especially how God intended for you. God doesn't just want you seeking it (peace), but he said you should pursue it (1 Peter 3:11). The word pursue connotes action; it will need you to act and make sure to do whatever it takes or in your power to have peace, especially peace that cometh from God in your life.

The fact is that experiencing God's peace is freely given and should be freely received because it is worth the while. So, are you ready to experience God's kind of peace? Peace like a river? The peace that will permeate your heart? The peace that will elude all understanding? The peace that will be soothing? The peace that can still keep you sane in an insane world? Then you need to take action. You can use the following wise words to begin your journey into enjoying the peace that cometh from the almighty God alone.

Acknowledging God is the beginning of the journey to experiencing God's peace in your life. When you acknowledge God in your life, then you are automatically surrendering to the authority of God. The good news is that God doesn't forsake those that know his name and acknowledge it. All of his promises will surely come to pass in his children's lives.

Psalm 100:3:

"Know ye that the Lord he is God: it is he that hath made us, and not we ourselves; we are his people, and the sheep of his pasture."

The scripture has instructed us to know God to be counted among his pastures. Being counted among his pastures means that all the promises, including giving you his kind of peace, will be bestowed upon you. God never goes back with his words; whatever he promised, he does it. He cannot lie; there is no atom of a lie in him; only the truth of his word. If God says he will do it, I can rest assured that he will do it. I do not have to make sense of it (Numbers 23:19).

All you need do to enjoy the spoken words of God is to acknowledge him as your father by being born again. You cannot bribe God, and he doesn't need your wealth or luxuries, but by being pure in body and spirit and keeping to his commandments.

Just like in your normal life, where you acknowledge your earthy father and make him feel important, you make him realize that you can depend on him and can trust his word of promises. You go to remind him about his promises about your life. It is the way God wants you to acknowledge him as your heavenly father so that his promises will all be yours.

Philippians 4:7

"And the peace of God, which passeth all understanding, shall keep your hearts and minds through Christ Jesus."

The peace we seek is the kind of peace from God that can't be comprehended by man's knowledge, standard, or ideas.

It defers all human wisdom, and it can't be compared to any peace that would be gotten from anywhere else. It can't be explained with any form of enlightenment and lots more. So, it is more spiritual than physical, which will be astonishing when you start experiencing it. So, it will be foolhardy of you not to embrace this kind of peace that is freely given that all you need do at this point is acknowledging God as your father.

I know the countless times I have had sleepless nights because of the myriad of issues that get stuck in my head. It keeps me tossing and rolling on my bed. I think of solutions that don't seem to bring me closer to the desired result, but I had to tell myself I need to acknowledge God in this situation and that he must have known about these issues before they had reared their ugly heads. So, let me allow him to take control of them while I have my peace.

Isaiah 46:10:

"Declaring the end from the beginning, and from ancient times the things that are not yet done, saying, my counsel shall stand, and I will do all my pleasure:"

To enjoy peace even in difficult situations, I acknowledge God that he will better handle the situation, pushing me into a rest and peace position like a river takes over. You know you are only get covered when you are under the shield of a certain thing. The same is applicable here. You can't acknowledge mammon or any other deity and expect to enjoy the peace that cometh from God.

John 10:27-28:

"27 My sheep hear my voice, and I know them, and they follow me:

28 And I give unto them eternal life; and they shall never perish, neither shall any man pluck them out of my hand."

Acknowledging God alone means that you are giving him an expressway to take over any distress calls in your life; he is taking over whatever will cause you sleepless nights. He is fighting whatever wants to take away your peace of mind even in turbulent situations. He is there to calm the storm so that you can still enjoy your peace.

Jesus and the Disciples were in a boat, and Jesus was said to be fast asleep in the basement of the boat when there arose a great storm that took away the disciples' peace. (Mark 4: 35-41). What did the disciples do? They acknowledged the fact that Jesus was with them and went to wake him up for help. Jesus immediately woke up to calm the raging storm, and he said, "Peace be Still" what happened next? We are told the wind ceased, and there was a dead calm.

This is the whole essence of acknowledging God in your seemingly hopeless situations; he will always come through to give you that peace you deserved. When the raging storms of life come to threaten your peace, call on your father. Father! You have given me the authority to decide how I feel. I speak peace to my mind, I speak peace to my body, I speak peace to my finance, and I speak peace to everything that troubles my soul.

So how can you rightly acknowledge God in your life so that you can start enjoying his peace that surpasses every understanding? You can achieve this by acting by his words and commandments.

HAVE NO OTHER GOD

God doesn't want you having any other God before or after him.

Exodus 20:2:

"I am the Lord thy God, which have brought thee out of the land of Egypt, out of the house of bondage."

Like you cannot disrespect your earthly father but running after other fathers or even acknowledging them more than your real biological father. It is the same way that God wants that same reverence from you; flee from every other god. It makes no sense running after dead gods that their gifts are temporary. Yes, Satan and his agents have their gifts, which might look real, but it is a mirage and adds more misery. However, if you want the peace that flows like a river, which is unending and never runs dry, you need that of God, the almighty, and the everlasting peace. You have to have only Yahweh, the only true God, and stand with him alone.

BELIEVE IN HIS POWER

To acknowledge God means you must believe in God.

Acts 16:31:

"And they said, believe on the Lord Jesus Christ, and thou shalt be saved, and thy house."

This is another goodness you will enjoy when you believe in God. The peace he will give wouldn't just be for yourself, even for the members of your family too. God is more than able to calm the raging storms in your life and put you in that place of rest you need. Believe that he can do it and leave it there at his cross.

Cast all cares upon him because Jesus got you. Always know that there's absolutely nothing God cannot do. You have to believe and go about your business every day in the truth that you have the peace of your Father in Heaven.

SURRENDER TO HIS AUTHORITY

How do people acknowledge gods? It simply by letting them know you are loyal to their leadership, right? The same is applicable here, you can't want a good thing from God, and you don't submit to his authority.

You have to let God know he is your all and all. You are for him, and he should do with your life has he likes. Of course, the thoughts from God are only thoughts of good. As you surrender, he will give you the peace you need, the peace that passeth all understanding.

Start acknowledging God today to experience God's kind of peace.

Chapter Two

Ask God for His peace

Enjoying the peace of God is one thing that you need to experience, you know why? Because the peace of God is the foundation of peace in every other area of your life. Isaiah 9:6 recorded that Jesus is the prince of peace, and he is one with God.

John 10:30:

"I and My Father are one."

The scripture means that asking to experience God's peace from God is the same as asking from Jesus, his son, the custodian of peace, and the prince of peace. So, if you seek to enjoy the peace of God that surpasses all understanding, the incomparable peace, the peace that can't be bribed to receive, the peace that will make you lie in permanent rest even in the face of adversities, then you need to ask of the Father.

John 16:23:

"And in that day ye shall ask me nothing. Verily, verily, I say unto you, Whatsoever ye shall ask the Father in my name, he will give it to you."

All you need do to enjoy the peace you need, the God kind of peace is for you to ask God, using the son's name he loved so much who is Jesus Christ. Asking God for his peace is one action you need to do daily because your heavenly father needs you to communicate to him daily about your life.

John 16:24:

"Until now you have asked nothing in My name. Ask, and you will receive, that your joy may be full."

You see, God knows all about your needs, he isn't blind, deaf, or dumb to your need of peace, but he needs you to draw closer and communicate it to him.

Edwards left for medical school without getting the cheque for his fees from his father. He forgot due to the excitement of passing the entrance exams into the medical school since he got the news two days before his departure.

When Edward got to school, he realized that his school was far away from home, and all he needed to do was put a call to his father and ask about the cheque. He became busy with other things that were more pressing at that time; he was almost running late because the portal for fees payment was almost closed, then he put a call again across to his father. He called the father and was shocked to realize that the cheque has been with him all the while.

The father said he had put the cheque in his old pajamas, and since he didn't call earlier to ask about the cheque, he felt he had seen it long ago. Edwards thanked the father and told him he got carried away with other things and forgot almost every day to call until he was running late. He checked the old pajamas, and there was the cheque. This is the same as you wanting to enjoy the peace of God. You need to start asking God about it.

Mathew 6:8:

"Therefore, do not be like them. For your Father knows the things you have need of before you ask Him."

The next verse instructs that you need to pray and ask for what you need. This simply means that God knows your every need, and he is ready to supply them. But you need to ask of him. Like in the example stated above, Edward's father knew too well that his son would need money for his fees, so he was proactive about it, even when Edwards didn't ask, but the father knew and did what a loving father should do. Immediately Edwards asked, he was told how to get it. So same applies to the love your loving father in heaven has for you. He said in

Mathew 7:7-8:

"7. Ask, and it will be given to you; seek, and you will find; knock, and it will be opened to you. 8. For everyone who asks receives, and he who seeks finds, and to him who knocks it will be opened."

All you need to do to enjoy peace in the chaotic world is to ask God for his peace to enjoy.

Asking God for anything through prayers is one way for

you to receive whatever you need from God. We don't have what we need because we don't ask God what we need (James 4:2-4).

You need to continually ask in prayer whatever you need, especially that of peace that the biggest Liar, Satan, tries to rob you of. Nothing can bring confusion, lack of peace of mind, chaos, and anxiousness like lack of peace. It can make you go mad and begin to nurse negative thoughts.

A typical example was when peace eluded the household of Job. It got to the point that the wife told him, "curse God and die." This is what Satan tries to do so that you wouldn't enjoy the peace that God has promised his children, peace like a river and one that surpasses all understanding. You don't need to give in to the tricks of the devil; rebuke him vehemently and begin to ask God today to calm all storms in your life and leave you only in his peace to enjoy. What would have been more wonderful than this? A father is just demanding his children to ask for whatever they need to receive.

Like I have already stated, freely, God's gift is given, freely will you receive. So, let not your heart be troubled when confronted with situations that try to take your peace away. Ask God to restore peace and that you want to enjoy the peace that can't be eroded by things happening now or things yet to come.

So now that you know the next action to take when looking at enjoying the peace of God, which is through asking God, you may ask what the right way to ask God is. As stated in the bible, don't ask amiss, which means doing it right or properly. You should do the following proper things to ask God rightly for peace.

START WITH THANKSGIVING

You should first thank God for other things he has done in your life. Let him know you appreciate him a lot. Our father loves to hear from you, how grateful you are for the tinniest of things you have been able to receive from him. So, you need to continually thank him for every gift you have received that you can and can't buy with money.

Like it is popularly known, prayer moves mountains, but praises move God. So, if you need God to move speedily for you, grant you that peace that will give you rest in all situations, then start praising him.

PRAY ALL THE TIME

God admonishes you to pray in and out of season. The only way to communicate with your father daily is through prayers.

You need to be in constant connection with God. You can't buy peace with all the wealth you have. Solomon first tried this; he gathers all the wealth he could and just wanted his spirit and soul to enjoy. But in the end, he realizes that they were all striving after the wind. So, to have peace in a mad world, where activities and situations only bring lack of rest, hypertension, and stress, you only need to enjoy God's kind of peace to live better.

1Thessalonians 5:17:

"Pray without ceasing."

Always remember that God is ready to supply all your needs according to his riches in glory, which peace is inclusive. So, harness your power of prayers and ask God for peace that passeth all understanding to enjoy it. So, pray without ceasing

HAVE FAITH IN GOD

Having faith is the most God wants from you when you ask for anything.

Hebrews 11:6:

"But without faith it is impossible to please Him, for he who comes to God must believe that He is, and that He is a rewarder of those who diligently seek Him."

So, you need always to believe that you will receive whatever you ask of God. Faith is the assurance of things hoped for, the conviction of things not seen (Hebrews 11:1), so you don't need money or luxuries to enable God to move for you; all you need is to exercise your faith, reignite your trust in God and believe that the storm will be over and calm will return.

You have to hold on because even in the Well, it is well. So, move by faith and not by sight and tell yourself whatever life throws at me, I will continue to enjoy the peace of God, and it shall be so.

Chapter Three

Stand on God's promises

A need in your life is there for you to rely on God's promise for that need wholly. Experiencing and enjoying peace in God is one of God's promises in the Bible.

John 14:27:

"Peace I leave with you, my peace I give to you; not as the world gives do I give to you. Let not your heart be troubled, neither let it be afraid."

So, you see, he has promised, and he will surely do it. God is no man that he should lie; neither is he a son of man that he will fail. He has told us always to hold him to his promises. God is ever faithful and to fail any mortal, and you aren't an exception. The promises made by God are his bond, and nothing can change it. He has expressly said that his words will never go back to him until there have accomplished what was promised.

Isaiah 55:11:

"So, shall My word be that goes forth from My mouth; It shall not return to Me void, but it shall accomplish what I please, and it shall prosper in the thing for which I sent it."

This scripture tells you that God's words must be fulfilled in your life, no matter how the devil tries to rob you of it. Why? Because God looks to see that his words are fulfilled in the lives of his children. Enjoying the peace of God is reminding God daily of him promising to give you rest even in bad situations. If you see good things for yourself, for your family, for your business, then know that you have seen well because God is always alert and active to perform his word (Jeremiah 1:12). You should delight in a God that doesn't promise what he cannot deliver; our God is more than able.

I know it can be difficult to embrace God's words when

all you encounter daily is tension and nervousness, but you should draw strength from the sea's actions. The sea rolls in at a point; it can surge high against the rocks and then surge out again with powerful force and before you know, everywhere is stable again — This is how you should view God's word concerning your peace.

The lion may roar, the dog may bark, and all sorts might happen, but God's word admonishes you to hold your peace. God will fight for you while you be at peace (Exodus 14:14). What battles are you confronted with? What has dominated your mind that you have lost your peace? Peace be still I speak to your inner man. You can only get a peace that is lasting, deep, and inexhaustible from God. At this point, you just need to hold him to his words.

Sonia, a lady with a pretty daughter that she dots on, just wanted her daughter to turn right, and she consistently used the weapon of promises. She will tell her little daughter that I will get you this or that if you never become naughty, excel in your academics, and you continue to exhibit good character, etc. Well, the little girl had to do a lot of things right if she needed the promises of her mum to come through. She reminds the mum and urges her to keep to her promise when the mum wants to deviate. Well, the mum had no choice but to make her words her bond. She just has to fulfill her promises. It is a win-win situation while the mother has a well-behaved child because of keeping to her words.

The child gets compensated because of obeying the mother and doing and following the instructions of her mother. Well, the whole idea of reminding God about his promises might sound weird. Of course, you will say, "Isn't he God, and all-knowing?" but also remember, reminding God of his promise of peace makes you show strong faith in God, that he can do it for you. That if he promised you his kind of peace, then you should receive it, and nothing should rob you of it. Note that reminding God of his promise to leave you in his peace doesn't mean that God had forgotten, NO! It isn't a passive reflection; rather, it is a bold act of calling God's truth into your present life.

Just like the story of Sonia's mum trying to encourage her little girl to do the right thing through her promises, it's the same thing God's love does to us. God's promises are energizing: they give you courage, and this courage enables you to get moving and doing only what you need to do.

Reminding God of his promise of peace in your life comes with a lot of benefits to all aspects of your life. You know lack of peace, and an unwholesome mind can badly affect your health, social life, mind, body, etc. So, when you start enjoying the peace of God, you will benefit a lot in your life. With God's kind of peace that he offers while you hold fast to his words, you will be having a new sense of inner happiness and bliss. You will be free from all nervousness, worries, and stress of life. You will have the ability to be more tact, patience, and tolerant. You will handle your daily affairs of life more effectively, efficiently, and better concentrate on life's most important things. You will be bestowed with a sense of power and inner strength; falling asleep easily and even sleeping soundly will be your portion.

So, with these numerous benefits that you will enjoy for just holding on to God's promise concerning your peace of mind, why don't you go into action to start enjoying the peace God has promised?

It is pertinent to always hold on to God's promise of peace in your life. You will need to let him know that you have that strong connection with his words so that his promise will be fulfilling in your life. If you need God to begin to perform his promise of peace in your life through perfecting his words, then you should take the following action.

PRAY TO GOD CONCERNING HIS WORD

If you need to remind God about his word, you need to pray to him. Praying is the right channel to get through to God to alert him that you want to enjoy his peace as promised.

Philippians 4:6-7:

"6. Be anxious for nothing, but in everything by prayer and supplication, with thanksgiving, let your requests be made known to God; 7. and the peace of God, which surpasses all understanding, will guard your hearts and minds through Christ Jesus."

So, reminding and holding unto God's promise of peace is for you to communicate with God, telling him to remember his promise of peace for you in all situations.

MEDITATE ON THE SCRIPTURES

There are so many scriptures on God's promise of peace in the Bible that you can meditate on for them to permeate your heart, and you will begin to see yourself living in the blissful place of peace. When you do this, you will get closer to having your desire. It will help you stay in faith and be more determined to achieve your aim. It will help you be reformed and direct your energy to the positive, enjoying the peace that only God can give.

Psalm 119:148:

"My eyes are awake before the watches of the night, that I may meditate on your promise."

So, you need to look up to God while meditating on his words to grant you peace that can only come from him to start enjoying his peace.

TRUST GOD CONCERNING HIS PROMISE

How else will you please God to fulfill his promise of peace in your life other than trusting him and believing that he will do what he said he would do? The scriptures gave an insight into how God keeps to his promises when you trust him with his words,

Joshua 10: 8:

"And the Lord said to Joshua, "Do not fear them, for I

have delivered them into your hand; not a man of them shall stand before you."

When God gave this promise, Joshua trusted it and went on to do the miraculous. Joshua trusting God's promise, went ahead to request that the sun should stand still upon Gibeon and the moon in the valley of Aijalon. The Lord kept to his word of promise and did as Joshua had desired, and we are told the sun and the moon remained that way until they won the battle. So, trust God to make his words concerning your peace of mind come to pass.

To enjoy God's peace, continue to stand and hold on to his promise, and he will give you your heart desire.

Chapter Four

Submit to God's Will

How else would you want to enjoy God-given peace, the peace that transcends all understanding, the peace that brings calmness to your spirit, body, and mind, the peace that supersedes all earthly situations without submitting to the Will of God? God always wants his children to submit to His Will and letting things go the way he wants. (Mathew 6:10) admonishes us always to make a prayer like this *"Your kingdom come. Your will be done on earth as it is in heaven."* Of course, you know that the Will of God can only be in your favor and not against what you desired as a child of God. Submitting to the Will of God means that you acknowledge God's freedom, God's supernatural being, and God's responsibility.

Charles Spurgeon asserted, "A man is not far from the gates of heaven when he is fully submissive to the Lord's will." You will receive whatever you asked of the lord when you allow his Will to be done.

You don't need to entangle yourself with what you can't disengage yourself from when you need the Will of God to be done in your life. All you need do is to learn how to bring your Will into submission and obedience to the Will of God on a practical, daily, hour-by-hour basis.

Ecclesiastes 9:11:

"I returned and saw under the sun that— The race is not to the swift, Nor the battle to the strong, nor bread to the wise, nor riches to men of understanding, nor favor to men of skill; But time and chance happen to them all."

So, you see a lot of things you need in life, including wanting to enjoy the peace of God isn't about your might, goodness or righteousness but it is according to whom God wants to bless or according to God's Will, which can only be good. So, you need to submit to His Will and grant your desire to find peace permanently in him.

You should note that inordinate desires mainly produce irregular endeavors. If your desire isn't kept in submission to God's providence, then your pursuits will scarcely be kept under the restraints of his precepts. You don't need to twist God's arm for you to have his Will of peace in your life.

Isaiah 59:1:

"Behold, the Lord's hand is not shortened, that it cannot save; Nor His ear heavy, that it cannot hear."

This scripture tells you that after asking God for his kind of peace in your life, you should still leave it to his Will because he has heard, and he will do it as he pleases, which will suit you better. One day, one of Jesus's disciples asked Jesus to teach them how to pray like John taught his disciples. Jesus taught us to pray to our father in heaven and let God's will be done as it is in heaven (Luke 11: 1-2).

Your prayers for finding peace in God should show submission to the Will of God. As already stated, the Will of God concerning your peace can't be compromised by situations of life, Satan, or his agents, and as such, you should allow God's Will to be done. You don't force God's Will concerning your peace. The time, how it will happen, how he will want it for you, and other things like this, but one thing is sure, his Will concerning you enjoying the peace he promised is sure. You have to allow his Will to be done, which is God's sovereign rule, while you submit totally to it.

Jesus was about to take up the biggest challenge of his life; to be crucified for the sins of the world, to experience the painful death on the cross. As the hours drew near for his death, Jesus withdrew from his disciples to a secluded mountainside in the Garden of Gethsemane. As a child who has taken up a man's physical body (flesh and blood), he knew he needed to acknowledge his father because he needed help from him. So, Jesus went to his father in a submission manner. (Mathew 26:39) reveals this He went a little farther and fell on His face, and prayed, saying, *"O My Father, if it is possible, let this cup pass from Me; nevertheless, not as I will, but as You will."*

This demonstrates how desperate Jesus wanted the cup of suffering he was about to drink to be taken away from him, but he still humbly surrendered to God's Will by saying, not my Will, but yours be done. When Jesus did here was willingly placing his desires in full submission to God's Will. As believers, we are to model after Jesus. When we are overwhelmed with the struggles of life and peace of mind is far away from us at that moment, choosing God's Will over our own need for peace at that point might not be easy, but the best thing will be to pray and leave the rest to God to do.

The truth is you can't bend God's Will to get what you want, so you should only seek God's Will concerning getting his peace then align it with his desires for you. You can't tell if God wants you to learn a lesson or two about your situation before getting into his peaceful state. Don't try to hasten things; just enjoy the ride as you journey into God's kind of peace.

They are rewards for you as you submit to the Will of God concerning wanting to enjoy peace from him. Firstly, you will have God's way, which will be the best.

Philippians 4:7:

"and the peace of God, which surpasses all understanding, will guard your hearts and minds through Christ Jesus."

Obedient to God's word gives you peace that is beyond understanding. You do not have the right explanation because the peace comes during storms of life, and it makes people wonder how you can be in a storm and exhibit so much peace. Why? Because you are obedient to God's word (Luke 11:28)

You may be wondering how do you submit to the Will of God as you seek and want to start enjoying his peace? Take the following actions not only enjoy the desired peace you need but get blessed more by God.

BE OBEDIENT

The first step to submitting to God's Will is obeying his words. Obeying his words doesn't mean that God is a tyrant that forces his words or ways on you. No! Far from it. The truth is that God is a loving father, and he wants the best for you. To enjoy his gift, you need to obey him. The power of life and death is in your hands, but God says you should choose life. By obeying God and choosing life means you are obedient to his words, and you will enjoy the life of peace that surpasses all understanding as he had instructed (Deuteronomy 30:19).

BE HUMBLE:

Pride goes before a fall. You just have to kill pride to be able to submit to God's Will. God dislikes pride and doesn't want his children to be proud. God will hear you from heaven if you humble yourself and seek His face (2 chronicles 7:14). Seeking God comes down to submitting to his Will.

Telling God, let thy will be done in my life concerning every chaotic situation means you are leaving it all to God to have his way. In this case, no arm-twisting, no forceful action, no coercion, no bad-mouthing, nothing at all, just humbly leaving it to God to sort it out, and you just enjoy the soothing peace he is bringing your way.

RELY ON GOD

How else would you show your submissiveness if you don't show by your action that all you have got is God by relying solely on him? You submit to the Will of God by leaving the want of peace or enjoying it to him.

Psalm 4:8:

"I will both lie down in peace, and sleep; For You alone, O Lord, make me dwell in safety."

You don't need to do much to enjoy the peace of God, rely on him, and submit to his will. As a believer in Christ Jesus, you have been called to a life of faith. A life of faith seeks to rejoice and be joyful in Christ Jesus. When we love and thankful through the storms of life, it is the ultimate demonstration that we rely on God's peace.

Our peace as Christians is not based on what we see all around us; it is based on the truth of God's word (2 Corinthians 4:18).

In seasons when we need the peace of God, it's often challenging to believe that God is with us. When we feel helpless and cannot mutter the right words as we ought, we can always rely on God's unfailing words that he will keep us in perfect peace. You can rely on God in the season of storms.

Chapter Five

Trust in God always

The secret to enjoying the peace of God is an open one; it is made known to people that seek it just like you are doing now. When you begin to trust God with all your heart, every good thing comes to you, including peace. Having peace in this insane world might be a bit of a struggle and sometimes might even elude you. You might even begin to believe that peace can be found in temporary circumstances, people, or places, but you should know that the ultimate giver of peace you seek is God. Leave all your unknown problems to a known God.

The God of heaven is known, and he never forsakes those that ever trust in him. He will give you peace, nay, perfect peace if your mind stays on him (Isaiah 26:3).

Looking at the life of the troubled man Jesus met as he journeyed alone helping people (Mark 5:1-20), the bible recorded that Jesus met a man who was troubled with an evil spirit, which causes the man to be in constant distress.

He was living in the graveyard. When people try to bind him with chains, he will break free, and he will go about destroying things and being very fierce. But when Jesus met him, he took away the evil spirit tormenting him and gave him peace as well as made him whole. You might be going through some life's struggles that take away your peace, especially those you can't do anything about. You need to trust God to take them away and give you the peace you need.

Romans 16:20:

"And the God of peace will crush Satan under your feet shortly. The grace of our Lord Jesus Christ is with you. Amen."

Trusting in God for your peace helps a lot in promoting

your health, which is the biggest aspect of your well-being. The truth is that when you aren't enjoying peace, maybe because of the turmoil and agony of life, your body system will begin to react negatively.

It has been found out that the immune system, nervous, cardiovascular, and even the endocrine interacts negatively when you are troubled (this will hurt your physical being). You know many health issues come from poorly managed psychological and emotional problems like abdominal pain, common cold, headaches, irritable bowel syndrome down to low back pain.

Many people are dying from one form of sickness or the other, and a lot emanates from life's struggles that brought a lack of peace. This is why God admonish you in (Philippians 4:6-9) to stay free from worries and anxiousness since they are twin evils that can ruin you. Do you know that God designed you to operate on trust? Yeah! That's the truth. Though we are limited in power and knowledge, our trust in God is limitless.

Putting your trust in God isn't easy, but at the same time, it isn't complex too. You have to believe that the all-powerful God is great enough to grant your heart desires according to his will.

The scripture says since we have been justified by faith, we have peace with God through our Lord Jesus Christ. Through Jesus Christ, we have also obtained access by faith into this grace in which we stand, and we rejoice in the hope of the glory of God. This revelation shows that God's soul-soothing peace that is freely given and his wondrous grace is available to you who place is trust in the Lord Jesus as your savior and Father (Romans 5:1-2). Trusting in God will open the way for you to enjoy the peace of God. It is the surest way to a life of peace that God has promised.

Trusting God and receiving his blessings, including enjoying his peace, goes hand and hand (Proverbs 3: 5-6). When you trust God, he will make sure not to disappoint you. He will not forsake you because he will look to make sure he honors your act of obedience and grant your heart desires. If you trust in the Lord with all your heart, he will direct your path; this includes directing you to how you can enjoy his peace and be in it permanently.

There came a time in my life when I was extremely poor. I couldn't pay my rent, had no money for food and suffered ulcers because I couldn't eat nutritional foods. My mum was also sick, and It looked as if life was meaningless because of financial problems all around. I didn't know what to do because I was tired of job hunting and even got to the point that there wasn't even motivation to apply to job opportunities. However, one thing I didn't let go of in my life was fellowshipping with other believers. I attended an evening service one day, and the word's theme was "Taking a rest in God." This theme was directly speaking about my situation.

The preacher admonishes everyone to take action through the words of the scripture. He said all we needed to do is trust God for our rest from all we were going through. He quoted Mathew 11:28, *"Come to Me, all you who labor and are heavy laden, and I will give you rest."*

The preacher assured us that the words of God never lie, and as such, we can trust it with our lives. What did I do? I left the issues that I couldn't handle at all to him, trusting that he would sort them out better. Did God do it more than I had expected? Yes! That's what he did. He brought help where I never expected, and peace was what I was experiencing while he miraculously sorted out the issues. I look back to date, and I keep wondering how I overcame that period without breaking down. This is what trusting the almighty does. Your heart's desire will be granted miraculously so that peace wouldn't elude you even while in the process.

If you want to enjoy the peace of God, then you need to trust God (proverbs 3:5-6). No matter how chaotic your life is right now, you should trust God to give you that peace that you can enjoy in the midst of all that. So how can you trust God even in an insane world to enjoy his peace?

DO AWAY WITH WORRIES

When you worry about your problems, then it shows you doubt God. The scripture says in (Mathew 6:27), can any of you add a single cubit to his height by worrying?

A worry is like a rocking chair that moves you forth and back with no concrete solution. So, don't worry about what you can't change. Leave it to God; trust him to do a better job with your situation. Just trust God.

TAKE A DELIBERATE DECISION TO TRUST GOD

I know it can be difficult to trust those you see physically, let alone God that you are yet to see. But you still need to make a conscious effort to trust God if you want him to move in your favor and grant you the life of peace you want to enjoy.

Corrie Ten Boom should convince you with his words, "never be afraid to trust an unknown future to a known God." So, take that decision today to only trust God for your peace.

ONLY HAVE POSITIVE THOUGHTS

Dwelling only on the positive shows your level of trust in God. I know how I have my peace whenever I see only the positives in a very bad situation. I know I have a big God I can trust, so I look only at the positive side of things.

Enjoying God's peace needs you to only be positive in your thought while trusting him to enable only positivity in the situation too. The truth is, the more you believe and trust God, the more limitless possibilities you experience in your life.

I will leave you to ponder on the words of Joel Osteen, "When you really believe, when you're in peace, you're showing God by your actions that you trust him."

Meditate on this and start trusting God to enjoy his kind of peace."

Remember, to trust in the Lord is to believe in who he is and the efficacy of his promises. In other words, to have confidence in, to be convinced of, to have the kind of assurance that produces the right actions.

Our discernment, knowledge, and understanding are limited to help us through life. Trusting in God gives us access to live life to its fullest. No life is more loaded than the Zoe life, the same life that Christ has. Trusting in God is not to be in denial of the realities around you. It is not about being in a bubble that everything is perfect when it isn't.

Trusting in God is a life committed to being in obedience to the Words of God when we go through difficult times.

Chapter Six

Flee from Sin

One thing that can hinder you from God's blessings, which includes enjoying his peace, is when you live in sin. I hope you know that the wages of sin is death; it might not just be a physical death but deadness in many areas of your life. Paul the Apostle admonishes in (Romans 8:1) that a condemned person will lack peace because that signifies punishment or trouble, and a troubled mind can't enjoy peace, especially the one not coming from God.

In Christ Jesus, there is no condemnation for you, and as such, you are wholly going to enjoy his peace, but the snag is that you need to live a life of purity. (Mathew 5:8) made this very clear that only the pure in heart shall see God. So, if you want God to come into your life and leave you with his kind of peace to enjoy it to the fullest, then you must leave the life of sins.

Going through life as a believer must be intentional — You cannot be merely existing. Sin brings guilt, and guilt steals our inner peace. A life bound by sin is never the plan of God for you.

John 16:33:

"These things I have spoken to you, that in Me you may have peace. In the world you will have tribulation; but be of good cheer, I have overcome the world."

This scripture simply means that your father is willingly and more than able to give you the needed peace you desire, but you need to live in holiness to behold his presence. You need to take action, consciously flee from what will hinder his presence in your life, which living in sin is one of them.

God anointed Saul to rule over his people, but one thing is that he wasn't living by God's words sent to him through Samuel. He totally disobeyed God and lived-in sin, and the spirit of the Lord departed from Saul, and an evil spirit troubled him. And Saul's servant said to him one day; you have many things troubling you, instruct me to get someone who can give you good music so that you can cheer up again (1 Samuel 16:16).

This lack of peace is what one goes through when one commits a sin or lives in sin. It separates God from you because the Holy Spirit cannot live in a sinful person, and neither can it operate in such a life. Enjoying God's peace though it is freely given comes with you taking the right actions instituted by God. God hates sin but not the sinner (Eccl 12:16) because when you sin, it is a transgression of God's word, and God has expressly stated that whoever sins must die.

Look, even if you aren't dying physically, you might still not be living well as offered by God. When you continuously live-in agony, pains, disappointments, fear, anxiousness, sorrow, problems, etc., you can't have peace, especially God's kind of peace, which surpasses all understanding. Without living and enjoying the peace of God, you will be living in self-denial if you think you are enjoying your life.

The Bible talks about the story of the prodigal son. He

felt he could enjoy the same peace outside his father's domain (Luke 15:11-32). He insisted that he needed his part of the father's wealth and that he could take good care of himself out there. It was like a coming of age for him; I can do it all by myself. There are times in our lives when we think we have got it all together; that we think we do not need God, that we have enough resources to go live life without the protection and the covering that comes with being connected to the father.

At such time, just know the enemy is setting up for an epic life of failure. Well, the prodigal son was granted his heart desire, and he left the father's covering. However, it gets interesting. It wasn't even long that he became troubled when he had squandered all he had, and peace of mind eluded him. He started experiencing conflicting thoughts on how he could get himself out of the situation that has now taken away his once-peaceful life in his father's house. This place of emptiness is the same thing that happens to you when you leave the covering of your Creator.

God will always give you your space when you disobey Him. You always have the power to choose what you want. Life or death? Peace or distress? Joy or sorry?

However, God has given us insight into what is best for us. He says, choose life that you may live. Yeah! For sure, God can't be struggling with other gods to take preeminence in your life. It would be best if you allowed him into your life willingly. How can you achieve that, in a simple term, "flee from all sins." You want to have and enjoy God's peace, then do what is right in his sight and obtain peace from God and man.

Proverbs 16:7:

"When a man's ways please the Lord, He makes even his enemies to be at peace with him."

This scripture is so apt! Do you know that poverty is your enemy? That Frustration, pains, disappointments, betrayal, and all other negative issues that take away your peace should be alien to you? They are supposed to be your enemy as a child of God. If you are going through all of these that have stopped you from enjoying the peace of God, then you need to go back to the drawing board.

(Isaiah 55:12) reveals that you shall go out in joy and be led forth in peace; this is what God has promised you, so if you aren't walking or living out these words, then know that you aren't enjoying the gift of God as promised. You need to search your heart and purge yourself of sins that are preventing you from enjoying the peace of God.

If you are ready to start enjoying God's peace that only he can give, you need to pursue righteousness, which means fleeing from sins. It might not be easy, but it is doable, and it is the best thing to do. You can take the following actions to live in purity.

DELIBERATELY LEAVE SINS

To be deliberate means being proactive to leave sins. It's like making conscious efforts to leave sins. You deliberately want to live a holy life to please God. The truth is that you will know when you are about to sin though you might have two spirits fighting to convince you of the action to take, always listen to that little still voice urging you to leave or flee from committing it. That's always the voice of God telling you to stop, so stop immediately.

ALWAYS ASK GOD FOR FORGIVENESS

The truth is that we have a merciful father. He is always willing at all times to forgive us.

1 John 1: 9:

"If we confess our sins, He is faithful and just to forgive us our sins and to cleanse us from all unrighteousness."

What else do you need to enjoy the righteousness in Christ Jesus than confessing your sins and denouncing them? If you are ready to enjoy the peace of God as promised, then go to your creator with a contrite heart.

Tell him about all the sins you have been living in. He is faithful to forgive. Tell him to purge you of them. In the Bible, God says, come and tell me what the matter is all about, come, let's settle it. Don't hide from me; be vulnerable. Though you think you are far too gone, I will want you back (Isaiah 1: 18). There is no place too deep that God cannot bring you out from. The prodigal son went back to the father, and when the father saw his son afar off, the father ran to kiss him. So, humble yourself before God and have his peace.

PURSUE RIGHTEOUSNESS

Pursuing righteousness means living a holy life. It is not about going back to sin and afterward to confess again.

Romans 6:1:

"What shall we say then? Shall we continue in sin that

grace may abound?"

Yes, you are right that our father is ever ready to forgive, but it will be irresponsible of you to continue repeating maybe a particular sin, always going back to confess to God. That means you do not seek true repentance. You are making a mockery of God, and the Bible says God is not mocked. You will be making a mockery of yourself here. The mercy of God is eternal, as you know, but God is not mocked; whatsoever a man sows, that is what he will reap.

Pursue holiness; don't be lazy when it comes to pleasing God. Guard your thoughts to only do what is pure and holy, and you will see the hands of God move swiftly in your favor, which is enjoying his peace without limits.

Chapter Seven

Seek the Favor of God

Being favored by God means enjoying a lot of unmerited blessings. It goes further to you having the ability to do something which isn't humanly possible. Many people wake up daily, get blessed daily not because they merit them or have done anything spectacular, but because God has favored them. The same can apply to you. You can request from God an undeserved favor to give you peace that will be soothing and calm. This kind of blessing can only be by the grace of God and the love he has for you.

Requesting God to favor you to enable you to enjoy his

ultimate peace means that God is in accord with you and has gracious kindness towards you. This is all about grace, which the bible described as unmerited favor. The truth is you might not earn it nor deserve it or even have the ability to attract it. You have to request that God show you favor and grant you the grace of enjoying his peace in all areas of your life.

Romans 9:15:

"For He says to Moses, 'I will have mercy on whomever I will have mercy, and I will have compassion on whomever I will have compassion."

This scripture shows that God can choose to favor anyone despite whom or what the person is; he is under no obligation to do it or rely on any criteria to decide. He will favor you despite all you have done or yet to do. So, the best action is leaving it at his feet and just believing you will find favor in his sight to experience the peace he had promised.

In the book of (Esther 2: 8-9), Young Esther found favor in the king's sight even as a poor orphan. When the king's edict had been proclaimed, many young women were brought to Shushan's citadel and put under the care of Hegai. Esther also was taken to the king's palace and entrusted to Hegai — who had charge of the harem. She pleased him and won his favor. Immediately he provided her with her beauty treatments and special food. He assigned to her seven female attendants selected from the best place in the harem.

When Esther went to the king, she asked for nothing other than what Hegai, the king's eunuch who was in charge of the harem, suggested. And Esther won the favor of everyone who saw her. She was taken to

King Xerxes in the tenth month, the month of Tebeth, in the seventh year of his reign. It happened that the king was attracted to Esther more than any of the other women, and she won his favor and approval more than any of the other virgins. This story is how favor works, you don't have to do anything other than just enjoying what God has allowed to happened or given to you, and the good news is that nothing can ever stop it from happening.

Requesting to be favored by God to live you in his atmosphere of peace is you having the faith of thought to let go of what you thought would happen and only embracing what God brings your way. The fact is it might be a twist, a turn, or a shift, but God has a plan for you, and it is most definitely better than yours. You can't be evil or be a worker of iniquities and expect to be favored by God.

Though God chooses to favor who he will, you have to allow God into your life by living a worthwhile life. Going contrary to God's will is sabotaging the grace that Jesus said abound for everyone who knows him.

Ephesians 2: 8-9:

"For by grace you have been saved through faith, and that not of yourselves; it is the gift of God, not of works, lest anyone should boast."

One good thing about requesting to be favored by God to experience His peace is that being granted this request comes with other positive outcomes. Having peace benefits you in different aspects; the same applies when you asked God to favor you to grant you peace. With you being favored, it will help produce honor for you amid your adversaries. Of course, in the first place, what brought the lack of peace is the adversaries. When you are experiencing the peace of God, you will be honored even in the midst of it. You will have great victories amid great impossibilities.

Having calm in adversity is what peace from God does; it will make you victorious even in a seemingly difficult situation. The peace you experience will conquer all negative thoughts, and you will receive supernatural increase and promotion. The truth is nothing brings more increase than peace in all aspects of our lives. There will be a lot of radiation, bloom, and flourishing.

Joseph, the son of Jacob, is another good example of one that requested to be favored by God as recorded in (Genesis 39). Even when he was sold into slavery by his brothers, it is recorded that he requested God to favor him in a strange land still. God did, and he was favored. Joseph's story is an epic story of God's favor. In prison, he was so at peace to see the problem of others. He was always willing to help other inmates. Due to Joseph's peaceful nature, he was recognized even in prison, which earned him the grace of being moved from prison to the palace.

God didn't only favor Joseph; the favor of Joseph even spilled over to the house of the Egyptian's ruler. The Lord blessed the Egyptians house for Joseph's sake: The Lord's blessing went with him everywhere he went (Genesis 39:5). In the house and the field, Joseph was blessed. Have you ever experienced this kind of favor before? You start a job at a company, and everyone seems to be of good cheer when you are around. The spirit of favor that produces excellence within you gets to everyone who interacts with you. You are the go-to person when clarity is needed in tough times. When everyone is agitated, they look to you for calming words of wisdom.

So, are you ready to request to be favored by God for his peace? Then you should take the following actions to attract God's favor. These actions will help to speed up things for you.

BE HUMBLE AND MEEK

Numbers 12:3:

"Now the man Moses was very humble, more than all men who were on the face of the earth."

You need to show humility as you request before the Lord to favor you. Humility was a weapon used by Moses; he was humble before God, and God favored him and decided to meet him face-to-face, which he never did for any other person. So, you are to do the same to cause God to work in your favor for your peace swiftly. Every day when I go out, I ask God to favor me. To order my steps and give me opportunities to serve others and learn from my day.

LOVE AND WALK WITH GOD INTIMATELY

How else will you want a loving friend to look upon you with favor other than walking with and loving him genuinely? Intimacy delights God. Intimacy is not about religious duties and demanding requirements. You do not have to change yourself before you commit to Him; He just needs you to come as you are, acknowledge that you need Him, confess your sin to Him, recognize you need to be free from sin, and accept His gift of forgiveness that Jesus Christ offered on the cross for you through his death and resurrection (Matt. 27:1-66, 2 Cor. 5:21). After asking for your sins to be forgiven, go ahead to talk to Him, and experience Zoe.

BE OBEDIENT

Sometimes, we can feel like our obedience to God gets us nowhere. However, obedience shows that God's love is in us, and we trust Him, which in turn releases God's power in our lives. Genesis 50 gave the account of this, Joseph who became the favored son of Jacob, went through difficult times, from being hated by his siblings, got sold into slavery, went into Potiphar's house, and was falsely accused and then landed in prison. Still, with all of these, he was favored by God because he was obedient, which enabled him to experience victories at every stage of his journey.

When you obey God, you will be blessed in your going out and in your coming in. Your obedience to God brings blessings and protection upon your children. Your obedience to God helps you stand out and abundant prosperity. You don't need to overstress yourself.

God will still bring you the needed peace as you hold unto him. So, go ahead to request to be favored by God to and grant you his peace today, and he will (Deuteronomy 28: 1-14).

Chapter Eight

Pursue Peace

I can remember a very popular song that my pastor love to sing during his ministration. The lyrics are *"Don't seek for peace when you work against peace, even though God freely gives peace."* You can't be asking to enjoy the peace of God when you don't give others peace or do things that will bring chaos into your life. You need to love peace to attract the peace of God.

Hebrews 12: 14,

"Pursue peace with all people, and holiness, without which no one will see the Lord."

This scripture is a commandment you need to follow if you seek to enjoy God's peace. The truth is you can't be giving trouble or be a troublesome person and expect to find peace. No! You attract what you are and give. If you want to see God in your life as the ultimate peace giver, then you must be a peace lover.

You need to fervently and passionately be in pursuit of peace to experience the peace of God. Peaceful people show peace, and it is a fruit of righteousness (James 3:18).

You can see the reason why you should be aggressive in pursuing peace. You will certainly be rewarded with bountiful blessings. Pursuing peace signifies a state of tranquility and harmony in one's relationship. This goes further to mean a state of not having an unresolved conflict or trouble with people around you. You might not be aware, but God wants you to be an aggressive pursuer of peace with all men in his wisdom.

Wanting to enjoy the peace of God means that you shouldn't allow conflict to fester unresolved in your life. It still points in the direction of loving God; you can't love God and hate your fellow men. Likewise, you can't seek to enjoy the peace bestow on men by God without being at peace with others.

The relationship between Merlin and Dave was frustrated by Dave's parents; they didn't seem to like the family Merlin came from in Wythenshawe, Manchester. To Thomas, which was a popular royal family, the idea of marrying anybody because you happened to love them doesn't sound right to them.

They believed royalty must get hitched to royalty. They didn't want a girl from a basic home with no surname to get married to any of their sons. Though Merlin had the best education since she met Dave at the prestigious Harvard College and could hold a lot independently, Thomas, Dave's parents, needed their son to get married to a girl from royalty.

So, they didn't give the two young love birds any peace. Being the head of their local assembly facilitating unit, Merlin took this problem to their district pastor. She was told to do only one thing to experience the peace that only God can give in her relationship: to be at peace with her would-be in-laws. Though it wasn't easy for her, her peaceful mien was reciprocated with harshness and rudeness, but she kept at it. She kept also asking God to give her peace as she was a peace-loving person. It got to the point where Dave's parents threatened him.

He was told, "If you get married to her, never come back here again." But they got married and moved into a new home despite the opposition. God did grant the couple the peace they needed; they were at peace and felt good about the union. Then the couple's first son came along after a year, and Dave's parents had no choice but to accept their grandson.

The few months rancor had ended, and peace resumed or took over. This initial union that met with lack of peace and stiffness was wholly accepted without much resistance, and the union is blessed with four beautiful children now. When you are at peace with others, even in difficult situations, God will cause you to enjoy his peace because you are keeping to his words of being at peace with your fellow men.

Do you know God rewards those that pursue peace? Yes, he does! The scripture says God blesses those who work for peace, for they will be called the children of God (Mathew 5:9). If you want to enjoy God's peace, which is a blessing from God, and then you need to do what will attract this blessing to you. You should be at peace with everyone and be even a preacher of it to others; maybe living by example will be your greatest teaching weapon.

You need to strive for peace with everyone that you may enter into the peace of God, put away rash gestures, harsh words, and malicious response talks that are directed at causing conflicts. Like Ted Twain's rightly stated, "When a conflict is brewing, we should assume it is avoidable and do everything to pursue peace."

I have been enjoying the peace of God for years now because I try to broker peace at all turns. After all, I know war is very easy to start. The world itself isn't mild to people, making people more unpleasant to one another.

Sometimes, I believe it takes a conscious effort to be peaceful because of the world's chaotic nature, but you still need peace. So, what do I do? When I'm confronted with harsh situations, I first sought for peace. I have realized that a better result is obtained when issues are sorted peacefully, so I go through the peaceful route to get things done. It is either peacefulness or nothing.

When I act with a peaceful disposition, I get a better

answer, and peace still reigns supreme in my life. So, I keep at it because of its benefits and the reward from God.

If you haven't been trying, then you should start experimenting with it today. I tell you; you would be regretting why you never thought it out this way before now.

Are you ready to start pursuing peace? To enjoy the peace of God, be on the path of peace. You would be glad you did. If you are having it difficult or looking for the right actions to take, you can use the under-listed ways to get it right.

LIVE ONLY IN PEACE

This statement simply means peace should be your watchword. You need to wear peace as your garment.

Be gentle as a dove and shun all things that will want you to war or have any conflict with anyone, especially for those you can avoid. Try to be in peace with those that want to fight you, only hand out peace even when others don't, never seek revenge or be angry with those that don't want you to have peace (Romans 12:10).

Try to live peaceably with everyone. Don't reciprocate any harshness from anyone. Note the words of Alinco Nero "Peace requires a rigorous, disciplined commitment to being quick to listen, slow to speak, and slow to become angry." It isn't easy, but it is doable.

To leave with others peacefully, you need the Holy Spirit to help you. The Holy Spirit helps us to handle conflicts with others when they arise. Many times, people get on our nerves, the very last nerve. However, we need wisdom from the Holy Spirit to live in peace with others, be willing, and always ready to serve and help them.

As believers, we are called to forgive those who may have offended us yet are unaware they need forgiveness from us. We must not expect that those who have offended us will come around seeking forgiveness. We must always be ready to let go of any offense easily and quickly.

RUN FROM CONFLICTING SITUATIONS

Like I have earlier stated, life is chaotic, so never you think for a minute that you wouldn't be faced with conflicts and disturbing situations.

The possibility of chaos is why the bible says to strive or pursue peace. You will be confronted with issues that would want to take away your peace or make you not to live in peace with others. But you can do it this way when the conflict is brewing; you should assume it is avoidable then do everything possible to pursue it with peace. Yeah! You might say this is hard, especially for unavoidable ones, but you can also see this as a form of spiritual warfare and endurance, which you strive to win. So, don't allow the devil to win. Still, make peace despite the situations and get the reward from God as a peacemaker. You will live in God's atmosphere of peace.

PRACTICE RESTRAINT

Practicing restraint is one skill you should master; you need to train your tongue, fists, and body language to resist an attack.

James 1:19:

"So then, my beloved brethren, let every man be swift to hear, slow to speak, slow to wrath;"

You need to refrain from using anything within you to cause discomfort to others. Expressing yourself is one freedom you have, but you must handle it with care even when you are right in a situation that might cost you your peace.

Restrain from exploding with accumulated complaints, frustrations, or disappointment. The tongue is one part of you that can cause mayhem in a twinkle of an eye. You need to be very cautious when using it. So that peace can still be maintained.

Chapter Nine

Act peacefully

You do not preach peace and fight with everyone that is not in agreement with you. Mathew 15: 8: "These people honor me with their lips, but their heart is far from me." You cannot enjoy the peace of God when your action and inaction don't connote peace. Acting peacefully is an action you need to take every day in your life. It isn't just a spoken word that needs to be told to others while we do otherwise.

The truth is that peace is one beautiful gift from God, and this justifies the fact that living a good life bears great fruits which peace is one of them. Of course, acting peacefully comes with a reward from God. Philippians 4:6-7 promises that the seed whose fruit is righteousness is sown in peace by those who make peace. Again, deceit is in the hearts of those who plot evil, but those who promote peace have joy.

These are the promises inherent in the holy book and can only apply to those who act peacefully, and God's peace, which he has promised, will be their portion.

The truth remains that a thing begets another. When you decide to be someone who seeks peace, you open yourself to less stress. Try always to seek reconciliation rather than quarrel. Where there is no peace, you lose the ease within you.

Do you know favor can only locate a peace-loving person? I have seen a young man promoted to a more prominent position because he is always a peacemaker. Whenever there's a chaotic situation in his office, he doesn't want to know who is right or wrong. All he wants is for everyone to be at peace. He needs only peaceful actions around him, which makes the working environment very conducive. He never knew that his director was taking note of this aspect of his life. Even when more qualified staff could take the position he was promoted to; the director felt he needed a more peace-loving person who acted peacefully and with decorum.

When we exhibit peacefulness, we bring God's peace our way and attract other fruits from being a person of peace. There are benefits that you experience when you act with a sense of peace. One of which is that God's peace will abound with you. Also, you get to enjoy the peace of God in abundance as he has promised that his kind of peace surpasses all understanding. Actions that you exhibit when everyone is expecting you to look for a fight. Actions that don't allow you to lose your inner even if the world is going crazy.

Another benefit is that you would enjoy the fruits that come with acting peacefully. You would discover yourself, gain favor, radiate in God's only love, and gain newness in all ramifications. This inner calmness is what peace does to the body and soul. It makes rancor disappear, and you find yourself only in a total atmosphere of serenity, which can only come from a place of peace. You would begin to view things differently when you immerse yourself in peace.

Wayne Dyer asserted, "peace can become a lens

through which you see the world. Be it, live it, radiate it out. Peace is an inside job." Acting peacefully in a chaotic world needs an inner push, but the benefits are enormous. So get yourself together and start with little acts that promote peace. Start with your family, work colleagues, teammates, etc.

Remember that peace comes from within, so do not seek it without the Holy Spirit's help. You have to recognize that being a person of peace isn't an act of weakness. It takes strength to be the one who seeks a peaceful resolution to problems.

Ask God for help

Remember, you can do all things through Christ that strengthens you. As I had stated, life situations can be so overwhelming that practicing the act of being peaceful becomes a chore, but you need to still live above it. It would help if you asked the creator to build a new spirit within you to fight all temptation with peace. You shouldn't expect this on a platter of gold but believe that you can fight it. Ask God, and he is ever ready to stretch forth his helping hands to you.

Chapter Ten

Believe in God

Do you believe in God for a good job? Do you believe he can raise the dead? Do you believe him for a good spouse? Etc. Then you can also believe him for peace in your life. Believing God for a certain thing means having faith in God to bring that thing to pass in your life. It means you have a strong conviction that something is true and hoping it will be true. You need to have this strong confidence in God for him that He will grant you his gift of enjoying his peace, which can't be gotten from other gods here on earth.

John 20:31:

"but these are written that you may believe that Jesus is the Christ, the Son of God, and that believing you may have life in His name."

This scripture tells us what happens when you believe in God. You experience life and in abundance too.

Enjoying the peace that comes from God is living life devoid of frustrations, disappointments, stress, anxiety, panic, and all other negative energies, even circumstances that show these emotions happen to us.

You will be living in self—denial if you are not enjoying the peace of God that passeth all understanding, the peace that shields you from all the storms around you, the peace of God that keeps you in a bubble and wrapped in God's love.

When you believe God for a thing, it shows you are surrendered totally to him; to bring it forth his way and time. It shows your submissiveness to the efficacy of His Word. An act like this from you will be so pleasing to God. Believing God for his peace is requesting that God, which you have strong confidence in, will fill your life with his peace.

Nothing beats having confidence and never get

disappointed at the end of the day. I had a friend that always fled to my home anytime she was facing problems in her home.

Well, she had very strict parents that just wanted things done their way. They felt their only daughter should abide by their rules even when she was no longer a child; at least she could fend for herself since she just got a job post-degree. So, whenever she encounters one of those heated arguments with her parents, boom! She leaves for my place, and she never gets disappointed because she will have her peace away from all the naggings and unsolicited advice from her parents. So, the confidence that she can have the peace she wants at any time in my home increased daily, which helped me not disappoint her. So, this applies to your relationship with God.

When you keep on believing in God for the needed peace in your life, you begin to build confidence in God, and in turn, God will be steadfast not to disappoint you in granting you his enjoyment of peace.

Mark 9:23:

"Jesus said to him, 'If you can believe, all things are

possible to him who believes."

What does this mean? Simply put, to have the confidence in God that whatever you desire that is good for you will be granted thee.

You should know that God divinely performs in your life, so you should always look beyond your power or natural abilities. This truth is why God is God, he does only supernatural things, and as such, you can have solid confidence in him, more like relying on him for your desired peace. What have you spent your time thinking is no longer possible? I want to tell you today, it is possible. Healing? It is possible.

Restored relationships? It is possible. ALL THINGS are possible... all things mean all things, there are no exemptions. ALL is all.

Seeing and reading about God's miraculous deeds of calming the sea, healing the sick, raising the dead, turning water into wine, and waking you up every day should inspire confidence in you. You need to believe that you can have the kind of peace God has promised if you believe in him. Remember, God has done it before. He is still doing miracles every day. He is the same God

(Hebrews 13:8). If he granted the desires of the people of old, who believed in him, you should be rest assured that he will be the same.

I'm a typical example of whom God has granted his peace just by believing I can only get my needed peace from him, and I'm so enjoying it. I have always believed that I can't be disappointed by God, so I look out for his will in my life, and I can say without any reservation that the peace I'm enjoying now is only from God, and I have been enjoying it for years now.

There are some pointers you need to know about believing God for your peace. As you already know, God's peace is freely given, and God wants you to have this gift of his by just believing in him. (Hebrew 11:6) admonish you to believe that God is real. By this, you would be able to depend on only him for the peace that runs like a river and never runs dry. How else would you enjoy God's peace if you don't believe his spoken word concerning peace (Mathew 4:4)?

Remember, God said he would give you his peace, not as the world gives, so how will you enjoy this if you do not believe his words. Just like Joyce Meyer stated, *"As believers in Jesus Christ, our work is to believe while*

God works on our behalf," so you see, God doesn't want much from you; just believe in him.

Your belief in God is like a seed, you need to plant it in your heart, and God will give you the harvest at his appointed time. When you believe, when you are at peace with things around you, you are showing God by your actions that you have absolute confidence in him. So, it would be best if you kept believing in him.

Believing in God takes work just like in other things you are hopeful about concerning God. To get yourself to believe in God's words and believe him to enable you to enjoy his peace might not be easy for you. So, you will need to take some actions which will help put springs on your feet to propel you take and do the right things.

You can start taking the following actions:

LEAVE IT TO GOD

Believing God is letting God take absolute control; you just have to keep believing that his peace will come to you as you journey along. Enjoying God's peace is free, so leave it to him and keep believing that it is done already. Like Roger King rightly stated, *"if yesterday didn't end up the way you wanted, just remember God* created today for you to start anew. God gives the best to those who leave the choice to him".

I don't do anything else than believing God that he wouldn't disappoint me. So, I enjoy his peace daily because I know he will feed me with it. So, I just position myself to keep enjoying. You can achieve the same while you leave the rest to God.

HAVE NO DOUBT

Don't be a doubting Thomas until you see before you start believing. No! Whether you are experiencing it or not, start believing peace is with you already. Believing is like taking the first step even when you don't see the whole staircase. This truth was my stance when I first realized I needed the peace of God in my life.

I pictured it in my mind, and I know I will need to wait it out. Today, I'm grateful for it because the feeling is heavenly, and only God can make it happen.

James 1:6 says,

"But let him ask in faith, with no doubting, for he who doubts is like a wave of the sea driven and tossed by the wind."

WAIT IT OUT

Believing God for his peace requires you to wait it out for its manifestation. The scripture assures that blessings are for those that wait on God. You need to learn to wait for God's appointed time because it will surely come to pass. So, if you aren't enjoying his peace now, you just have to hold on and keep believing. Woodrow Wilson asserted that all things come to him that wait provided he knows what and who he is waiting for. These words are an absolute truth about waiting it out.

Here you have them, the different bullet-proof way by which you can enjoy the peace of God. You might not need to go through the whole process; you can just pick the comfortable points and act on them. I have been using each of them, and I can say without any doubt that they work like magic. It will be the same for you. So, get going with the pearls of wisdom mentioned here and continue living in the total atmosphere of peace.

A PRAYER FOR PEACE

My Father in Heaven, at times, I feel like I am at war, where the battle is close to home. I feel it within me.

Often, I go through storms that seem not to end — I am struck on every side, with confusing thoughts flooding my head. I admit many times fear creeps in to steal my peace. Lord, I need your peace — your peace that calms even the raging sea, your peace to speak calm to my distressed spirit. Lord, only you can give me that.

Lord, I know that to have your peace, I need to trust you to experience it. Today, I declare that I trust you. I am asking you to take the wheels and give me peace that makes no sense to me; peace beyond my understanding. Lord, I cannot control the events and circumstances, but I can allow your peace to be my anchor. Thank you for giving me this gift of peace and for every storm, you have allowed me to go through. I trust and thank you for your peace that is always with me. Amen.

ABOUT THE AUTHOR

Leon O. Newman is a multi-gifted Preacher of God's Word, motivational speaker, leadership coach, and author. He is the founder of the IAmPurposeful Initiative, with a vision to see that people live purposeful, meaningful and fulfilling lives.

With Thousands of people inspired by his IAmPurposeful Initiative (www.Iampurposeful.org) online portal, Leonard uses the Word of God to teach, equip, motivate, and inspire people to lead a life of purpose, love, faith, compassion, and victory in God. He is the Author of "**So You Failed, Now What? — Learn How to Thrive and Achieve Success in Life in Spite of Your Most Epic Failures**" and other life-transforming books on purposeful living, many of which continue to be a blessing to people.

Leon has often stated that many great preachers have influenced him such as Dr. Myles Munroe, Pastor Charles Omofomah, John Maxwell, Bishop T.D. Jakes, Pastor Sam Adeyemi, and many more.

He continues to seek ways to serve people and inspire them with the Gospel of our Lord Jesus Christ.

You can connect with him www.IAmPurposeful.org and read his Rhema Blog Posts on www.IAmPurposeful.org/blog

ONE LAST THING

If you enjoyed this book or found it useful, I would be very grateful for you to post a brief review on Amazon. Your support really makes a difference and I read all the reviews personally so I can get your feedback and make this book and future books even better.

Thanks again for your support.

Printed in Great Britain
by Amazon